AUTHOR OF *THE IDENTITY THEFT*

DEFEATING DEPRESSION

This Book is a Kiss from Heaven!

DOMINIQUAE BIERMAN, PHD

Author of *The Identity Theft*

Defeating Depression © 2011-2021 by Dominiquae Bierman

All rights reserved. This book may not be copied or reprinted for commercial gain or profit. The use of short quotations or occasional page copying for personal or group study is permitted and encouraged. Permission will be granted upon request.

Unless otherwise identified, Scripture quotations are from: *The King James Version* or *New American Standard Bible*. Used by permission. All rights reserved.

Published by *Zion's Gospel Press*

52 Tuscan Way, Ste 202-412
St. Augustine, FL, 32092
shalom@zionsgospel.com

Paperback ISBN: 978-1-953502-33-9
E-Book ISBN: 978-1-953502-34-6

On occasion words such as Jesus, Christ, Lord and God have been changed by the author, back to their original Hebrew renderings, Yeshua, Messiah, Yahveh, and Elohim.

Bold or italicized emphasis or underlining within quotations is the author's own.

Printed in the United States of America

First Printing December 2011, Second Printing June 2021

Dedication

This book is dedicated with all my heart to my beautiful, challenging and talented son, Yuval, who unbeknown to him in the midst of his suffering, inspired me to write this book. When he wakes up from his nightmare, he will realize that his life is a gift to many others and for the glory of God! May he always choose the principles written here!

"All your children shall be taught by YAHVEH and great shall be the peace of your children."
—Isaiah 54:13

TABLE OF CONTENTS

Chapter 1: Defeating Depression 1

Chapter 2: Fear & Depression 13

Chapter 3: Freedom from Pain, Lies & Depression 25

Chapter 4: Disappointment & Depression 37

Chapter 5: Family Curses, Demons & Depression 47

Chapter 6: Trust in God will Remove Your Depression . . 57

Chapter 7: "Love" – The Medication that Never Fails . . 61

Epilogue: Vessels of Clay 69

CHAPTER 1

Defeating Depression

"Anxiety in the heart of man causes depression, but a good word makes it glad."
—Proverbs 12:25

D epression from Webster's New Unabridged Dictionary means, "Low spirits, gloominess, dejection, sadness, a decrease in force, or activity, or amount, a decrease in functional activity. An emotional condition either normal or pathological characterized by discouragement, a feeling of inadequacy, the act of humbling abasement as a depression of pride. Abasement, reduction, sinking, fall, humiliation, dejection, melancholy."

Major Depression Facts

Major depression is the number one psychological disorder in the western world. (1) It is growing in all age groups, in virtually every community, and the growth is seen most in the young, especially teens. At the rate of increase, it will be the 2nd most disabling condition in the world by 2020, behind heart disease.* It is good to know that Yeshua (Jesus) provided a way out of depression when the Creator said about His Son:

"Surely He has borne our griefs and carried our sorrows."
—Isaiah 53:4

When He died for us on Golgotha in Jerusalem, He died for our salvation, healing and deliverance, and this includes depression!

Nearly everywhere that we go to minister, the LORD gives me a Word of knowledge concerning depression and suicide. Many people have been miraculously set free from depression and hopelessness as we bring forth the MAP Revolution Message to the nations. Sometimes people that have suffered from over 50 years of chronic depression are able to smile and rejoice for the *first* time in their lives!

One such case happened to us in Ecuador. As we were leaving from the Guayaquil airport after an intense time of ministry in Ecuador, some people came to bid us good-bye, and among them there was a middle-aged, toothless lady. She was smiling from ear to ear and had no front teeth at all! She made a considerable effort to come to the airport from a remote village and without any private transport. Her purpose for coming was to show us her "toothless smile" as

---

* http://www.clinical-depression.co.uk/Depression_Information/facts.htm

a sign of appreciation for our ministry. She told us that she had suffered from chronic depression for over 50 years and that she was healed under our ministry, and she could now genuinely smile and be happy for the *first* time in 50 years! Needless to say, we were overjoyed and tears ran down our cheeks as we received this marvelous testimony as a gift from heaven and as full reward for our time spent in Ecuador. What a privilege it is to make people *smile* and rejoice from their hearts after so many years of suffering!

In one of our meetings in Mexico, as I was asking for people to give their testimonies of healing, a young man came to answer the altar call for salvation, tears streaming down his face, as the LORD had healed him from depression right there on the spot. His testimony caused around 100 people to answer the altar call for salvation on that day! The lady that brought him to our meeting was *his own Christian therapist* that in desperation hoped for a miracle for her own patient! What medicine could not do, the Holy Spirit did it in a split second! To Him is all the glory forever!

I am not disclaiming in this book the use of drugs and medications in certain cases. Psychiatric help can be like a "lifeboat" to a drowning person. Some of my loved ones have been helped by medication; however, if you know the root cause of depression, you can live a life of freedom from this plague that is a major attack on modern day man.

My Own Testimony

It is in my weakness that YAH (the Lord) uses me in the area of depression as nearly every member of my immediate family has been plagued from depression, and one even committed suicide due to it. I have suffered the deep distress of catering to people in serious critical depressions and mental disease all my life. As I am writing these very lines, my own son, who is a soldier in the Israeli Army, is suffering from depression that has been caused by pressure and anxiety. As a mother, I am going through a very painful time, yet in the midst of my own pain I feel compelled to write this book so that all those that are suffering from depression can receive *hope* and a *way out*!

The Factors That Cause Depression

1. A family curse that is repeated throughout the generations due to *idolatry*, witchcraft, involvement in the occult, Kabala and the active membership in secret lodges such as the Free Masons, Odd Fellows, etc. It can also manifest as a "genetic chemical imbalance" (Deuteronomy 5:8, 28:28,29)

2. A root of bitterness, hidden anger and unforgiveness. (Matthew 18:34,35)

3. Fear, anxiety and stress (Proverbs 12:25, 1 John 4:18)

4. A serious disappointment in life, such as broken promises, divorce or a broken relationship, the death of

a loved one, or any frustrated expectation "Hope deferred makes the heart sick" (Proverbs 13:12)
5. Unresolved grief (Genesis 37:34-36)
6. Vitamin and nutritional deficiency
7. The use of Illicit mood-altering drugs and alcohol

Treatment For Depression

1. Repentance: In 2 Chronicles 7, we have the antidote for all sickness, be it spiritual, emotional or physical:

If My people who are called by My name will humble themselves, and pray and seek My face, and turn from their wicked ways, then I will hear from heaven, and will forgive their sin and heal their land.

—2 Chronicles 7:14

- Humility to recognize the need
- Prayer to seek YAH (the Lord) and inspect our hearts
- Turn from our wicked ways of mistrust and fear rather than faith, disobedience to God's commandments, and any unforgiveness and hidden anger. Forgiveness is a key issue, forgive yourself, others, and even God!

"For if you forgive men their trespasses, your heavenly Father will also forgive you. But if you do not forgive men their trespasses, neither will your Father forgive your trespasses."

—Matthew 6:14, 15

2. Confess your sins to someone you trust that has a

holy walk with God and have that person pray for you.

"Confess your trespasses to one another, and pray for one another, that you may be healed. The effective, fervent prayer of a righteous man avails much."

—James 5:16

3. Take the Word of God as medication.

"He sent His Word and healed them and delivered them from their destructions."

—Psalms 107:20

"My son give attention to My word, incline your ear to my sayings do not let them depart from your eyes, keep them in the midst of your heart, for they are life to those who find them, and health to ALL their flesh."

—Proverbs 4:20-22

Make for yourself a word prayer of at least 5-7 Scripture promises, declare and meditate on those Scripture promises day and night and at least 3 times a day! Record this Scripture prayer and listen to it while you are driving, speaking it out loud and also silently to yourself all day long.

4. Begin to obey God's commandments to you with no excuses

"The work of righteousness will be peace and the effect of righteousness, *quietness and assurance forever."*

—Isaiah 32:17

I will paraphrase from the original Hebrew:

"The actions of those that are made just by doing what is right in the eyes of God will be shalom, wellbeing and wholeness in every way; And those who worship Him according to His commandments (holy worship!) will be quietness and *absolute confidence forever.*"

The word *righteous* from the Webster's Unabridged Dictionary means, "Right in wise manner, upright, virtuous, acting in a just way, morally right, good, excellent, satisfying, pleasant, authentic, Godly, just, upright, virtuous."

Our righteousness comes from having been made right with Yah (God) through Yeshua's (Jesus) blood sacrifice, and it is to be followed by obedience to His Commandments and by a right walk with Him. When we are made right with Elohim through Yeshua, in a forgiven state we then begin a personal walk with Him, a walk of loving obedience to His commandments as written in our hearts by the Holy Spirit. (Jeremiah 31:31-33)

"If you keep My commandments, you will abide in My love, just as I have kept My Father's commandments and abide in His love."

—John 15:10

Walking in love, obedience and forgiveness is an antidote for fear and thus fights and defeats the torment of depression.

"There is no fear in love; but perfect love casts out fear, because fear involves torment. But he who fears has not been made perfect in love."

—1 John 4:18

5. Total trust in Elohim-God, His Word, His plan and His character. Trust is the antidote against anxiety, one of the major root causes of depression in the 21st century. Trust develops through continual prayer and meditation of the Word of God.

"Be anxious for nothing, but in everything by prayer and supplication, with thanksgiving, let your requests be made known to God; and the peace of God, which surpasses all understanding, will guard your hearts and minds through the Messiah Yeshua."

—Philippians 4:6, 7

This is actually a commandment – "Be anxious for *nothing*" and the way to achieve it is by:

Prayer, Supplication & Thanksgiving

Most people are anxious because they lead a prayer-less and unthankful life, so they are always revolving around themselves and their own problems.

1. Praise is an important key to release healing and the presence of *Yah*. (As in Halelu*Yah*)

"You have turned for me my mourning into dancing; You have put off my sackcloth and clothed me with gladness, to the end that my glory may sing praise to You and not be silent. O Yahveh my God, I will give thanks to You forever."

—Psalm 30:11-12

2. Inner healing is the key for inner soul and heart pain. Inner healing happens when we acknowledge the pain and let the spirit of truth and the Word of God bring light to the most hidden corners of our soul.

"Then Yeshua said to those Jews who believed Him, 'If you abide in My word, you are My disciples indeed. And you shall know the truth, and the truth shall make you free.'"

—John 8:31, 32

"The Spirit of Yahveh GOD is upon Me, Because Yahveh has anointed Me To preach good tidings to the poor; He has sent Me to heal the brokenhearted, To proclaim liberty to the captives, And the opening of the prison to those who are bound; To proclaim the acceptable year of Yahveh, And the day of vengeance of our God; To comfort all who mourn, To console those who mourn in Zion, To give them beauty for ashes, The oil of joy for mourning, The garment of praise for the spirit of heaviness; That they may be called trees of righteousness, The planting of Yahveh, that He may be glorified."

—Isaiah 61:1-3

Inner healing can happen when someone else prays for you, or when you pray and let Yah work on your soul to bring truth and light to your deepest painful emotions.

3. Conventional treatment – In some cases there is a need to receive conventional medication and drug treatment before a person can be settled enough to allow for God's word and spirit to work. In these cases, by all means receive treatment and then apply all the rest.

4. Deliverance from demons is an important part in defeating depression as in many cases there is demonic activity involved in depression; however, depression is not only caused by evils spirits, and it is important to treat the spirit, soul and body!

"Then His fame went throughout all Syria; and they brought to Him all sick people who were afflicted with various diseases and torments, and those who were demon-possessed, epileptics, and paralytics; and He healed them."

—Matthew 4:24

5. Nutritional supplements are very important in order to treat depression and most particularly vitamin B complex and Vitamin C; however, for a more thorough list, consult with a professional nutritionist and health consultant. There are also some herbs that can be helpful, such as St. John's Wort, Chamomile, Valerian Root, etc. It is also important to change your nutritional habits to healthy habits by decreasing white sugar, processed foods and chemicals, such

as nitrates and MSG.

"For thus says Yahveh GOD, the Holy One of Israel: 'In returning and rest you shall be saved; in quietness and confidence shall be your strength.'
—Isaiah 30:15A

In the next chapter, we will talk about fear and anxiety as a root cause of depression.

CHAPTER 2
Fear & Depression

"For God has not given us a spirit of fear but of power and of love and of a sound mind."
—2 Timothy 1:7

As I write this series on Defeating Depression, I am basing my approach on the assumption that Elohim-God is the creator of man, and therefore His Word has the final say about His creation. The Bible or the Word of God, as manifested through the Hebrew Holy Scriptures known as *Tanach,* or by some as the "Old Covenant" and through the Apostolic Writings, or also called the "New Covenant," is the Manufacturer's manual of instruction. It contains all the information for man's right functioning and wellbeing. In the same way that if we violate the instructions given in the manual of any expensive machine we could cause the malfunctioning of that machine and eventually its total breakdown and loss, if we violate God's instructions, it can cause the total breakdown of man.

Man is a much more intricate creation than manmade cars and other machines. Man is a unique creation and *only* the Creator knows all about the crown of His creation: *Adam*. Fortunately for us, He left us the manual of instruction: the Bible.

"He sent His Word and healed them and delivered them from their destructions."
—Psalms 107:20

I am fully aware that conventional psychiatry's approach is different than mine. Psychiatry sees the root cause of most mental illness a factor called "chemical imbalance." I see "chemical imbalance" not as root cause per se, but as an outcome of a deeper root cause. Psychiatry would prescribe medication to solve the situation, and I see medication as a possible "lifeboat" when people do not respond to reason, prayer and spiritual treatment. But even so, it needs to be followed by a retraining of the mind that would prevent such occurrences in the future. I see a mind transformation as the key for most, if not all, mental diseases.

"And do not be conformed to this world, but be transformed by the renewing of your mind, that you may prove what is that good and acceptable and perfect will of God."
—Romans 12:2

Fear and all its derivatives, such as stress and anxiety, are one of the major causes for depression.

"Anxiety in the heart of man causes depression, but a good word makes it glad."

—*Proverbs 12:25*

Fear and all its derivatives causes torment.

"There is no fear in love; but perfect love casts out fear, because fear involves torment. But he who fears has not been made perfect in love."

—*1 John 4:18*

What Is Fear?

- Fear is a demonic spirit that makes people crazy. This is a very tormenting fear based upon tormenting lies inspired by spirits of darkness that plague the mind with "scary scenarios." This demonic spirit can come in through watching horror movies, involvement in witchcraft activities and especially trauma.
- Fear is also a "fight or flight" reflex when in danger – this is a normal or even a "healthy fear" that can keep you from trouble, for example, it will make you function quickly if a car is about to run you over and thus save your life!
- The healthy "fight or flight" reaction activates the adrenal gland to secrete a large quantity of adrenaline, and in some cases due to trauma, it does not "shut off" and it keeps working over time, thus causing terrible distress and a constant state of *anxiety*. Sometimes it is triggered by "push buttons" related to the trauma in completely

unrelated situations. For example, a person that suffered financial collapse might become anxious in subsequent years whenever there is even a minor financial challenge that poses no real danger.

- Fear is also an emotion that can be caused by a real situation or by demonic spirits. Demonic spirits can work through trauma and past experience in order to create a vicious circle of negative thoughts. The more that the person thinks negatively, the more that the fear and the anxiety grow, thus affecting the chemical balance of the brain and causing a psychiatric disorder termed "Psychosis" which is characterized by terrible dread and by taking things out of proportion, imagining some devastating scenarios that do not exist, or even feeling physical discomforts with no evidence of disease at all. Depression can very often be accompanied with symptoms of Psychosis.
- The Fear of God is the healthy spirit, emotion and attitude that heals people from all other unhealthy fears.

"Do not be wise in your own eyes; Fear Yahveh and depart from evil. It will be health to your flesh, and strength to your bones."
—Proverbs 3:7-8

"The fear of Yahveh leads to life, and he who has it will abide in satisfaction; He will not be visited with evil."
—Proverbs 19:23

HOW TO TREAT DEPRESSION CAUSED BY FEAR

In order to treat depression that is caused by fear, stress and anxiety, there is a need to treat both the external symptoms of anxiety and dread and the root cause of the fear. In many cases, people develop harmful fear and anxiety because they are worried about their daily sustenance. What shall we eat? What shall we wear? How will we pay? What will my future be?

Yeshua warned us about that in Matthew 6:25-34:

"*Therefore I say to you, do not worry about your life, what you will eat or what you will drink; nor about your body, what you will put on. Is not life more than food and the body more than clothing? Look at the birds of the air, for they neither sow nor reap nor gather into barns; yet your heavenly Father feeds them. Are you not of more value than they? Which of you by worrying can add one cubit to his stature? "So why do you worry about clothing? Consider the lilies of the field, how they grow: they neither toil nor spin; and yet I say to you that even Solomon in all his glory was not arrayed like one of these. Now if God so clothes the grass of the field, which today is, and tomorrow is thrown into the oven, will He not much more clothe you, O you of little faith? "Therefore do not worry, saying, 'What shall we eat?' or 'What shall we drink?' or 'What shall we wear?' For after all these things the Gentiles seek. For your heavenly Father knows that you need all these things. But seek first the kingdom of God and His righteousness, and all these things shall be added to you. Therefore do not worry about tomorrow, for tomorrow will worry about its own things. Sufficient for the day is its own trouble."*

—Matthew 6:25-34:

So, the best antidote against anxiety is faith and trust in God's provision, His perfect plan for our future and of course obedience to God and to His commandments – "Seek ye first the Kingdom of God and His righteousness (His right way of doing things) and all these things shall be added unto you."

Miraculous healings of depression and all mental healing still needs to be followed by a complete program for mind transformation!

Mind transformations begin with salvation: PLEASE PRAY THE FOLLOWING PRAYER

> Dear Father in Heaven, I choose to put all my trust in You and in Your word and plan for me. Thank you for sending your Son Yeshua, the Messiah, to take my place as a sinner. Thank you Yeshua for dying for me that I may live! I believe in you and that you rose from the dead on the 3rd day, and I invite you to be my Master, Savior and Healer; please forgive me of all my disobedience and rebellion and teach me to walk with you. Thank you for making me free and whole to serve you all the days of my life. Amen.

Congratulations! This is the first step to come out of depression, put your trust in God's provision of salvation for you; salvation includes healing and deliverance from depression, it is all "in the package"!

Practical Steps to Follow:

1. Build yourself up in faith – Since faith and trust in God's provision is essential in order to maintain a healthy emotional life, it is necessary to build yourself up in faith.

"So then faith comes by hearing, and hearing by the Word of God."

—Romans 10:17

It is necessary that you constantly hear the Word which is the truth about God's faithfulness to provide for you in every way. Begin with making for yourself "word prayers" of at least 5-7 Scriptures that talk about YAH's (God's) unfailing provision for your situation. Read, meditate, melodize, think and declare those Scriptures day and night until you believe them. You will experience anxiety leaving you, and your faith will be built up! If you suffer from depression due to the fear of death or of sickness, then make sure that you have given your life to God through Yeshua and begin to meditate on Scriptures concerning healing and/or eternal life.

This book of the law shall not depart from your mouth, but you shall meditate in it day and night, that you may observe to do according to all that is written in it.

"For then you will make your way prosperous, and then you will have good success."

—Joshua 1:8

Since during depression your mind goes in vicious circles of negative thoughts, then changing the meditation of your mind will eventually turn around your situation!

"Finally, brethren, whatever things are true, whatever things are noble, whatever things are just, whatever things are pure, whatever things are lovely, whatever things are of good report, if there is any virtue and if there is anything praiseworthy— meditate on these things." —Philippians 4:8

2. Another way of building up faith is by prayer

"Be anxious for nothing, but in everything by prayer and supplication, with thanksgiving, let your requests be made known to God; and the peace of God, which surpasses all understanding, will guard your hearts and minds through Yeshua the Messiah."

—Philippians 4:6-7

This kind of prayer has the element of Petition b) Supplication c) Thanksgiving

When you have "prayed through," you will experience a great relief, and His peace, shalom, and wellbeing will flood your soul! The best way to make a petition prayer is by quoting His Word and promises to Him and then pleading with Him to manifest His promises (that apply to your situation) in your life, finishing with thanksgiving and praise for His grace and mercy! Remember, He does not 'owe" us anything, but He is committed to keep His Word. We are in constant need of His mercy.

This kind of prayer should be prayed as often as you feel anxiety creeping back. After you have "prayed through," leave everything in Yah's (God's) able hands!

3. Prayer in Tongues or in the Spirit

"But you, beloved, building yourselves up on your most holy faith, praying in the Holy Spirit."

—Jude 20

This is one of the main reasons of why it is essential to receive the Baptism in the Holy Spirit with the evidence of speaking in tongues, because it builds us up in our most holy faith. This is a *sure antidote* against depression!

4. Repentance from any selfishness, self-centeredness and any known sin in your life. Remember that He said that if you put Him and His kingdom *first*, everything else that you need will be added unto you with no stress nor striving.

5. Contentment and thankfulness

"Now godliness with contentment is great gain. For we brought nothing into this world, and it is certain we can carry nothing out. And having food and clothing, with these we shall be content."

—1 Timothy 6:6-8

Selfish ambition, covetousness and jealousy can cause terrible distress and unnecessary stress to run after things because "others have them." Of course, the end result of this would be depression. A life of praise to Yah (God) and thanksgiving is essential for mental health.

6. LOVE, LOVE, LOVE – Since fear is the *opposite* of *love* and *God is love*, your choice to love God and others (including your enemies!) at all times will keep you emotionally healthy all of your life!

"And his master was angry, and delivered him to the torturers until he should pay all that was due to him. 'So My heavenly Father also will do to you if each of you, from his heart, does not forgive his brother his trespasses.'"
—Matthew 18:34, 35

A lot of the fears and torments are connected with bitterness and unforgiveness. Forgive *everyone* at *all times* and for *every reason* and you will have a very healthy soul! When we forgive, we humble ourselves to be like Yeshua who forgave us when we did not deserve it. Unforgiveness is a form of pride and He said that He resists the proud:

"But He gives more grace. Therefore He says: 'God resists the proud, but gives grace to the humble.'"
—James 4:6

When you walk in forgiveness, you walk in love, and when you walk in love, fear flees and so does depression!

"There is no fear in love; but perfect love casts out fear, because fear involves torment. But he who fears has not been made perfect in love."

—1 John 4:18

7. Vitamins and nutrition – Fear and stress cause the body to be depleted of vital nutrients, such as vitamin B, vitamin C and Calcium. I strongly suggest taking a higher quantity of those during stressful times and to improve you nutrition with healthy foods. Again, ask your nutrition expert about these.

When Fear Is Caused Due to Demonic Spirits

Though all unhealthy fears are connected with the operation of evil spirits as well as the coping with some realistic problems, there are some situations of fear that are plainly demonic, such as fears caused due to the watching of horror movies and/or due to idolatry or witchcraft activities such as Ouija board séances, the contacting of the dead and other spirits of deceased people, and of course all satanic worship. In these cases, it is imperative that you go through a proper prayer of *deliverance* from demons by a qualified and trusted minister.

When a person is an unbeliever or is in a non-receptive state, the only treatment available against this kind of depression will be psychiatric treatment with some tranquilizing drugs, and even anti-psychotic drugs, accompanied with psychological treatment. As I said in my previous issue, I do not discard this kind of treatment when it is needed and nothing else works. This is a necessary "lifeboat" in some instances. However, I believe that most of the fear-related depressions can be overcome with the spiritual instructions given in this chapter.

In the next chapter, we will talk about depression due to lies that cause soul pain. In order to finish I would like to bless you with the prayer of 3 John 2, *"Beloved, I pray that you may prosper in all things and be in health, just as your soul prospers."*

CHAPTER 3

Freedom from Pain, Lies & Depression

"Yeshua spoke to the Jews who had believed him. "If you obey my teaching," he said, "you are really my disciples. Then you will know the truth. And the truth will set you free."
—John 8: 31- 32

My Testimony

The more that I write about the subject of *depression,* the more people that are "coming out of hiding." It is quite amazing to find out how many in the body of Yeshua are suffering from depression and are afraid of letting anyone know for fear of being judged by others. Many of those that suffer greatly are actually pastors and leaders, and they are even more afraid and ashamed to let others know, so they suffer in secret and sometimes even come to the verge of suicide! I fully understand; one time I suffered from depression for an entire year and hid it so well that even my husband didn't know. I would cry myself to sleep every night and only I and Yeshua knew of my loneliness and pain. Of course, I had real good reasons for my depression: my daughter had been sick for three solid years, coming and going from hospitals, and the last report of the doctor was 'that there was no hope'. Everyone would agree with me that this was enough cause for depression and sadness; however, I was regarded as so strong and full of faith by all that no one doubted my ability to stand under all pressure! However, I was falling apart and no one knew it! Fortunately for me, I have a really good relationship with Yeshua, and so I decided to retreat myself in my pastoral office for three days and three nights in order to find an answer from Him. The contents of this chapter are the result of my three-day prayer retreat from the 9th-11th of November, 2001. What the Holy Spirit showed me during those three critical days has changed my life, my ministry and my daughter, who is alive and well *forever*! My prayer is that it will also change yours!

"What hurts you, Dominiquae?"
When I entered the three-day retreat as I mentioned above, I sat before YAH (God) unable to do anything, let alone really pray! I just sat there and He asked me the question that has changed my life! "What hurts you, Dominiquae?" This question took me by surprise since I was not there to talk about my pain, but rather to get an answer of why was my

daughter not healed if I had been solidly believing, never faltered in declaring His Word, and was, in my eyes, obeying His will and serving Him? It did not make any sense to me to be 'punished' with losing my daughter to this terrible illness! However, God decided not to answer my question, but rather ask me one about my condition, about my pain! No one had asked me that question before, everyone was praying for Adi and for her situation and pain, but not for mine.

It took me a few seconds to react to this surprising question! But when I did, boy I did! "My motherhood is hurting me, LORD!"

To which He answered, "Write it all down, write all your pain, all your feelings down and do not try to be 'prim and proper', write from your guts, even if it's ugly!"

Ouch, I am not used to this; I only speak faith, who knows what will come out of my heart? This was scary, nevertheless, I obeyed my Master and Healer, and I wrote. I must have written a scroll or a small book, but I do not remember as I was crying too hard as I was writing. I was crying and screaming! Once it was all written, I felt an amazing peace, like 1000 tons had fallen off my chest; I could breathe again. But I was peacefully sad as I detected that on these pages, I had written what I truly felt about me, my daughter and God, and it was not pretty! Nor did it line up with His Word – in other words, in spite of my courageous faith stand I had believed many lies and thus was in tremendous emotional pain!

Emotional Pain

"My soul melts from heaviness, strengthen me according to your Word."

—Psalms 119:28

What is emotional pain? I would say that it is the hurt or pain that we feel inside because of what we believe about ourselves or about some traumatic situations that have happened in life. For the most part, our emotional pain lingers and becomes *depression* and other forms of mental illness due to our erroneous interpretation of traumas or hard circumstances. In other words, *if* we would get the true interpretation, then pain would leave and with-it depression also!

Denial is a 'safety mechanism' and its purpose is to keep the pain "hidden" pretending that it does not exist.

However, this works for a while, allowing the victim of that traumatic pain to live a borderline bearable life; however, all of a sudden, like in a pressure cooker, pressure builds up, and it begins to want to come out and erupt! It normally erupts in the form of depression, mental breakdown, psychosis, etc. Most people live in one or another level of denial. What the Holy Spirit did with me during my life changing retreat was to challenge my denial by asking me the surprising question, "what hurts you?" and then instructing me to "write it down" honestly. In other words, He had me blowing off my built-up steam in the security of His loving and accepting presence! Anyone that would take time off in His presence and do the exact same things will get the exact same results! You will feel like tons of pressure has fallen off you, and you will detect that you have been believing some lies that are contrary to His Word and will for you! The good news is that nothing is hidden from Him, so though this will be 'news' for you, it's *old history* for Him; He knows you inside out!

"O Yahveh, you has searched me, and known me .You know my down sitting and my uprising, you understand my thought afar off. You compass my path and my lying down, and are acquainted with all my ways."

—Psalms 139:1-3

If you can believe this, then you will have the courage to be what I call "brutally honest" when you express your pain on paper!

Lies & Erroneous Interpretations

I am going to make a statement here: "The more lies that you believe, the more pain that you will have. The less lies, the less pain. No lies, no pain."

"Yeshua spoke to the Jews who had believed him. 'If you obey my teaching,' he said, 'you are really my disciples. Then you will know the truth. And the truth will set you free.'"

—John 8: 31- 32

When we know the truth intimately, then we are free; freedom means no pain at all. Pain is an outcome of *sin*, our own sin and the sins of others against us. The *best news* that I ever heard in my life came to me during this retreat when Yah Himself said to me, "Dominiquae, I did not design you for *pain*!"

My answer was, "You could have fooled me, LORD! I thought that pain was my middle name!" Do you feel like I did? I have *great news* for you! The Creator did *not design you for pain*!

Now, go ahead and say it to yourself out loud! "*I am not designed for pain!*"

I did not say that we will not suffer; I only said that when the suffering comes, we are not supposed to hold onto and absorb the pain in order to carry it inside. He said clearly in Isaiah 53:4:

"Surely He has borne our grief and carried our sorrows."
—Isaiah 53:4a

He has already done it and is ready to do it every day, so how come we carry so much pain, grief and sorrow?

The answer was given to me during my retreat: I had believed lies about myself, God and my daughter's situation. I had interpreted some traumatic events in my life in a wrong way. I had come to the conclusion that I was the worst mother in the world, and I was trying to prove myself as a good mother by standing in faith for the healing of my daughter.

Since Elohim did not answer me, that proved the point that I was the worst mother, and on top of it, He hated me! Did I know all this in my conscious mind? NOOOOOO, I was a woman of faith, I only believed and proclaimed the Word! I did not acknowledge my pain or my suffering; I loved and worshipped God all the time, I was in denial! Deep within me I had pushed all these feelings of worthlessness and had put the 'lid' on them, the result of this denial was depression!

Does this sound familiar to you? Maybe you have gone through some traumatic events, such as death of loved ones, divorce, rape, abortions, bankruptcies or others, and you have pushed the pain down instead of acknowledging it and allowing the Holy Spirit to truly interpret them for you, the precious, awesome, all healing Word of God giving you the correct perspective? Do not despair – you are not alone; you can begin today!

"My soul clings to the dust, revive me according to your Word."
—Psalms 119:25

The Threshold of Forgiveness

As I was writing "The book of my pain" down, I felt terrible grief and terrible anger, but when I detected all the lies that I had believed, I moved from *anger* to *repentance*. I began to ask YAH's forgiveness, and I began to forgive myself, God and others that I thought I held nothing against. I had uncovered all the pain and grief in my heart and the lies that I believed were exposed to the light. My wellbeing was at hand!

"He that covers his sins shall not prosper: but whoso confess and forsake them shall have mercy."
—Proverbs 28:13

Declare Truth Over the Lies!

Once I finished doing that, the Holy Spirit told me to take a marker and highlight all the lies that I detected on the paper! That was a very relieving activity; the lies were now highlighted and *in the open*! They could not hide as snakes in the darkness anymore, and they could not "bite me." I did this with *gusto*! Then He told me to find a Scripture that opposed that lie and to declare it one time over the lie! The Word of YAHVEH is *so powerful* that it works better than a laser beam! Only one time of declaring His eternal word over the painful lies caused them to be *dismantled* in my mind and to leave me forever! And with it, *pain also left*!

"Your Word is a lamp to my feet and a light to my path."
—Psalms 119:105

Remember my previous statement?

"The more lies that you believe, the more pain that you will have. The less lies, the less pain. No lies, no pain."

I will add one more thing – pain functions inside of you as a *block* to the flow of the Holy Spirit and His glory, so:

"The more pain, the less glory, the less pain, the more glory. *No pain, all glory!*" So, this is the secret to an unhindered flow of anointing:

Get Rid of the Lies, Get Rid of the Pain, and Get Filled with His Glory!

After this three-day retreat, depression left me, and the glory of Elohim began to flow unhindered in me. My external circumstances did not change, my daughter was still as sick as ever, but I had changed! I also understood that I was to do *maintenance* every month. And so, every month I go on a 3-7-day retreat in order to maintain myself *free from lies, free from pain* and *free from depression*! Maybe you only need one day where I needed three days, but by all means do not delay to retreat yourself with Yeshua and follow the instructions of this chapter. You will thank Him and me forever! *You are not designed for pain*! While my daughter was not instantly healed but rather her condition grew worse, I had the inner fortitude now to keep going, and one and a half years later, she was released from the hospital in *full remission*! Today, she is a blooming flower. To our marvelous heavenly Father is *all* the glory!

Redirecting My Course

On the following morning, I came out to our morning prayer meeting, where the Holy Spirit showed me that I had broken my vow to be traveling to the nations. I had made that vow right after my salvation, but because of Adi's illness, I broke the vow for I was trying to rescue her, so in my mind I couldn't possibly travel anymore. As I said above, I could not heal her, not even after three years of standing by faith and declaring the Word. I had tried everything and nothing worked! But when I got rid of the lies, the pain and the depression, my ears were open to hear the rebuke of the Lord. I had forsaken apostolic ministry trying to 'save' my daughter. My husband told me later that no one could talk to me about this prior to my life changing retreat! I was too full of pain to *listen*! Now, after you are free from pain and depression, *listen* to His direction for your life. He will probably *redirect your course*. Be prompt to obey and live to the fullest of what He has designed you to do! I immediately began to travel again, in spite of my daughter's strong objection! Had I not obeyed Elohim's instruction, I doubt that she would have been alive today. Had I not rid myself of lies, guilt and worthlessness, I would have not been able to go in spite of all opposition from my daughter's side. Once you are free from lies, you will have new strength to stand and to obey. Once you obey, you will experience His back up, support and blessing. Remember to maintain yourself free from lies and pain at all times! The enemy will throw you 'curve balls' often but if you are free from lies and pain, you will come out on top at all times!

"And it shall come to pass, if you hear diligently unto the voice of Yahveh thy God, to observe and to do all his commandments which I command you this day, that the Yahveh your God will

set you on high above all nations of the earth. And all these blessings shall come on you, and overtake you, if you hear unto the voice of Yahveh your God."

—Deuteronomy 28:1,2

Freedom from pain will be freedom from depression and an unhindered flow of his abundant life and glory!

Remember the steps to follow:

1. Take time to have a prayer retreat, disconnect all phones ,and allow *no one* to interrupt you!

2. When you are in, dedicate it to the Lord and ask the Holy Spirit to help you find what hurts you.

3. Ask yourself, what hurts you?

4. Write your pain down in full honesty.

5. Weep and shout if you need to! Make sure that you are in a private place so no one tries to 'rescue you'.

6. Once you realize that you have believed lies about yourself, God and your situation, go into repentance and forgiveness.

7. Highlight the lies that you have detected.

8. Match Scripture against *every* lie and declare it once by saying: for example, "The following is a LIE: 'God hates me', the *truth* is that 'God so loved *me* that He sent His only son...." Remember that His Word works better than a laser beam, so use it against each lie; please be thorough!

9. You are FREE. Now praise Him for His deliverance!

10. Hide his Word in your heart and meditate on it *always*!

"*Your Word I have hidden in my heart that I might not sin against you.*"

—Psalms 119:11

11. Take time to *listen* to His instruction.

12. Rededicate your life to truth and freedom and to do His will at all times!

"*The entirety of Your Word is truth…and you shall know the truth and the truth shall make you free.*"

—Psalms 119:160, John 8:32

CHAPTER 4

Disappointment & Depression

"Hope deferred makes the heart sick."
—Proverbs 13:12

One of the major causes for depression is deep disappointment, the Word of God calls it "hope deferred"; in other words, a certain hope that never becomes a reality or that delays in materializing. Depression is exactly the opposite of expectation. In most cases, depression is accompanied by a sense of hopelessness or "what's the use." This feeling is normally based on experience, for example: "I have been praying for 18 years for my family to be saved and have seen no answered prayer," or "my husband has promised me thousands of times that he will change but he never does," or "God promised me through a prophetic word that I will do great things for Him, but I am still working as a simple clerk," or "I believe that by His stripes I am healed, yet my physical condition is not improved," or "I was hoping to have a great family life, and my marriage ended in divorce," or "I have done my best to reconcile with my parents, and yet they still reject me," etc. These are some of the many complaints of someone that has been deeply disillusioned by God, people and life.

When the disappointment goes deep enough, it causes a feeling of deep hurt, bitterness and then despondency; the attitude will be of great mistrust in Yah (God), His Word and people. There is a point where there are no more expectations of life and thoughts of death begin to plague your mind, some people even contemplate suicide, and all this is caused by *disappointment*. You expected something to happen that:

A) Did not happen and will never happen.

B) Did not happen in your time frame, and you believe therefore that it will never happen.

Your mind then decides to either cope with this reality in a positive way or to quit expecting anything at all. When it decides to quit, this is *depression,* and it can be dangerous.

Disappointments, Disappointments, Disappointments

First of all, let me make a statement here: disappointments are part of life as much as breathing and eating; all of us at one time or another will suffer some disappointments. The question is our choice of reaction when they come. There are some disappointments that need more processing than others, in every case, *processing is needed* and *denial is a killer.*

A disappointment is like walking through a dead end street. You expected to find an exit and you can't go on lest you turn around and find another way.

Disappointment From People

Since we are all imperfect humans, we will all disappoint someone at some time. So, we need to take into consideration that as much as people have disappointed us, we most probably have disappointed some people. In that sense, we are all in the same boat! However, it is necessary to process and to acknowledge the disappointment, the broken promise that has caused your heart to become sick. If you went through a divorce, there is a broken promise there; if your father or mother committed suicide, they have broken their promises to you; if they abandoned and rejected you, it is the same. Then disappointment and mistrust will set in.

Important exercise: Write down a list of all those that have disappointed you, broken their promises or broken your trust. Acknowledge your pain first and even mourn for the lost relationship. Then go ahead and forgive and begin your healing process!

Forgiveness

"Then Peter came to Him and said, 'LORD, how often shall my brother sin against me, and I forgive him? Up to seven times?'

Yeshua said to him, 'I do not say to you, up to seven times, but up to seventy times seven.'"
—Matthew 18:21-22

The only way out of depression due to the disappointment of people is *forgiveness*. Complete forgiveness and being willing to trust again. Unforgiveness and mistrust are a lot more dangerous than taking the risk of being disappointed again. Yeshua said if your brother sins against you, forgive him 70 times 7, in other words: endlessly! He knew that our loved ones were going to disappoint us and the antidote was *continual forgiveness*. Choosing to trust again is pivotal for recovery! It is better to take that risk than to live in the emptiness of constant mistrust. This is possible only if you trust God above men, because then you will know that He is able to heal you every time that people break your trust. What can keep us sane when people fail us is the humility to realize that we have also failed people many times and so we need constant mercy and forgiveness and second and third chances, so we are willing to extend that to others. Some people are too prideful, thinking that they are a lot better than others, and they fail to see that they too have acted sinfully against others, so they do not forgive and refuse to trust again. Pride and unforgiveness will keep you depressed!

"Also He spoke this parable to some who trusted in themselves that they were righteous, and despised others: 'Two men went up to the temple to pray, one a Pharisee and the other a tax

collector. The Pharisee stood and prayed thus with himself, 'God, I thank you that I am not like other men—extortioners, unjust, adulterers, or even as this tax collector. I fast twice a week; I give tithes of all that I possess.' And the tax collector, standing afar off, would not so much as raise his eyes to heaven, but beat his breast, saying, 'God, be merciful to me a sinner!' I tell you, this man went down to his house justified rather than the other; for everyone who exalts himself will be humbled, and he who humbles himself will be exalted.'"

—Luke 18:9-14

Disappointment in Yourself

If you are disappointed in yourself, you need to process it, acknowledge it and forgive yourself.

Important Exercise: Write down a list of all the people that you have disappointed, including yourself and God. Write down all the promises that you have broken to yourself and to others. Go ahead and *repent* by:

A) Asking God's forgiveness

B) Asking people to forgive you

C) Making a new commitment for change

Do not ever be afraid to *try again*. Mr. Edison only found the formula for electricity after trying 10,000 times and failing. He never gave up and he did not see the 10,000 futile attempts as failure but as "10,000 ways of how not to do it!" Finally, due to his tenacious perseverance, he succeeded, and due to that we enjoy electricity today! Had it not been for his positive attitude, you could not use a computer or read by a night light, there would be no high tech to speak about. Just imagine how much your life depends on electricity! So, yes, maybe you are not going to succeed right away, but *never quit trying!*

Forgive yourself and try again, *never stop trying* until your last breath! Life is *worth living* to the fullest even if there are many obstacles!

"The thief does not come except to steal, and to kill, and to destroy. I have come that they may have life, and that they may have it more abundantly."

—John 10:10

Disappointment in God

"For the vision is yet for an appointed time. But at the end it will speak, and it will not lie. Though it tarries, wait for it; because it will surely come. It will not tarry. "Behold the proud, His soul is not upright in him; But the just shall live by his faith."

—Habakkuk 2:3, 4

Many, many people are angry and disappointed with the Almighty. The reasons for this are:
- A) A) Expecting the Almighty to do things our way
- B) B) Expecting Him to do it in our time frame

Both of them are called *presumption*.

> *"Surely you have things turned around! Shall the potter be esteemed as the clay; for shall the thing made say of him who made it, 'He did not make me?' Or shall the thing formed say of him who formed it, 'He has no understanding?'"*
> —Isaiah 29:16

Presumption is rooted in pride and in our own interpretation of Elohim-God and of His Word and Ways. We need to separate between the written Word of Yahveh and His revealed Word. When He speaks a Word to you in your innermost being and even confirms it through a prophecy, then you can stand on it and believe for it, obey His instructions and wait *until* it comes to pass. Take into consideration that waiting on this word will test your patience and perseverance, and it will most likely not come to pass when you expect it. It will probably come "suddenly" – when you least expect it!

His written Word gives us many promises, and most of them are conditional, in most cases you will see the Word *if*.

> *"Now it shall come to pass, if you diligently obey the voice of Yahveh your God, to observe carefully all His commandments which I command you today, that Yahveh your God will set you high above all nations of the earth. And all these blessings shall come upon you and overtake you, because you obey the voice of Yahveh your God: 'Blessed shall you be in the city, and blessed shall you be in the country.'"*
> —Deuteronomy 28:1-3

In other words, you cannot expect them to come to pass unless you fulfill His requirements, and even when you do (at least in your own eyes), it will still happen in God's timing and not yours! If you do not understand these principles early in your walk with Yah (God) through Yeshua, you will have built up frustration, anger, disappointment and mistrust in Him, and eventually you will also suffer from some type of depression.

This is the dead-end street I had mentioned before; it really leads nowhere, so the only option is to turn and to find another way. This other way is the way of humility and trust.

Important Exercise

Write down in what manner YAH (God) disappointed or frustrated you. Forgive Him, ask His forgiveness for your pride, presumption or mistrust, forgive yourself, forgive others, and begin a new lifestyle!

"God is not a man, that He should lie, or a son of man, that He should repent. Has He said, and will He not do? Or has He spoken, and will He not make it good?"

—Numbers 23:19

Word Medication

Write down for yourself a *word prayer* about the faithfulness of God of at least five Scriptures and declare them day and night until they become part of you!

Disappointment & Depression

The prophet Habakkuk knew the secret of trusting Elohim at all times, even during the painful time of banishment and exile,

"Though the fig tree may not blossom, Nor fruit be on the vines; Though the labor of the olive may fail, And the fields yield no food; Though the flock may be cut off from the fold, And there be no herd in the stalls— Yet I will rejoice in Yahveh, I will joy in the God of my salvation. Yahveh God is my strength; He will make my feet like deer's feet and He will make me walk on my high hills. To the Chief Musician. With my stringed instruments."

—Habakkuk 3:17-19

When you choose the way of trust, though you may not see anything encouraging with your natural eye, you will enjoy His strength and His joy!

"Have you not known? Have you not heard? The everlasting God, Yahveh, The Creator of the ends of the earth, Neither faints nor is weary. His understanding is unsearchable. He gives power to the weak, And to those who have no might He increases strength. Even the youths shall faint and be weary, And the young men shall utterly fall, but those who wait on Yahveh Shall renew their strength; They shall mount up with wings like eagles, They shall run and not be weary, They shall walk and not faint."

—Isaiah 40:28-31

As you choose to trust your Father in Heaven against all odds, you keep persevering, forgiving and loving; you will never fail and depression will flee!

Trusting Elohim unconditionally is closely linked with the fear of God. When we fear Him, we will not consider breaking His commandments as an option, and we will know that we cannot exercise manipulation to make Him act; however, true faith and even desperate faith and trust will move Him. A person that fears Yahveh can also trust Him *fully*, thus he can walk completely *whole* in the midst of all circumstances!

"For you who fear My name the sun of righteousness will rise with healing in his wings."

—Malachi 4:20

May His healing break forth speedily for you as you apply these instructions!

CHAPTER 5

Family Curses, Demons & Depression

"You shall have no other gods before Me. 'You shall not make for yourself a carved image— any likeness of anything that is in heaven above, or that is in the earth beneath, or that is in the water under the earth;'"
—Deuteronomy 5:7,8

In the first four chapters, we touched on depression due to fear, lies, pain, traumas and disappointments; however, there are depressions that are "inherited" due the sins of our ancestors and family curses. In this case, we will see "familiar spirits" at work; those are spirits of darkness that plague entire families. Medicine calls it "genetic diseases." If the father or the mother suffered from depression and we see the same happening to the children, it will be labeled "genetic" and thus "inevitable". The Word of

God calls it *sins of the forefathers.*

"You shall have no other gods before Me. 'You shall not make for yourself a carved image—any likeness of anything that is in heaven above, or that is in the earth beneath, or that is in the water under the earth;'"

—Deuteronomy 5:7,8

If your parents or great, great grandparents up to the 4th generation before you worshipped gods other than Yahveh, the God of the Bible, then the *iniquity,* which is the outcome of their sins, will be visited upon the children. One of the most common expressions, of what I will call "family curses" due to idolatry, (Occult, witchcraft, membership in secret societies, Free Masonry, Kabala, etc.) is in the form of mental sickness and depression. In this case, the children are paying for the sins of their ancestors! This is a very painful, but Yeshua gave us a way *out*! He became a curse for us and paid the price for all our iniquities, however, receiving this marvelous gift is not automatic; it requires us to put our faith and trust in His finished work of sacrifice at the Roman Cross! In other words, we need to turn from worshipping other gods to worship the God of Israel only through His Son Yeshua, whom He sent to redeem us from all sin, iniquity, curses and mental illness!

"All we like sheep have gone astray; we have turned, every one, to his own way; and Yahveh has laid on Him the iniquity of us all."
—Isaiah 53:6

There are other depressions that are a result of the sin of witchcraft and idolatry in your own life. If you have been involved in any form of occult, witchcraft, paganism, or drug and alcohol addiction and even smoking, etc., you need to repent and cleanse from all its unrighteousness as there are demons that have been given legal rights into your life, and one of them is depression! Idolatry also functions through the use of superstitious objects, good luck charms, charms against the evil eye or the like. Also, whenever you worship or pray to any other but Yahveh, the God of Israel through His Son and Risen Messiah Yeshua. Prayers to Elohim through mediators like dead rabbis (a very common practice among Jews) or the Virgin Mary in all her forms (a very common practice among Catholics) are all forms of idolatry.

"For there is one God and one Mediator between God and men, the Man the Messiah Yeshua."
—1 Timothy 2:5

How to deal with family curses?

There is only one way to escape the vicious circle of family curses. It is by putting our full trust and faith in the *one* that paid the price and was made a curse so that we could be redeemed from the curse that has befallen us for breaking God's holy commandments. Yeshua became a curse Himself in order to rescue us from this terrible predicament!

"For all have sinned and fall short of the glory of God."
—Romans 3:23

To sin is to break Elohim's commandments, and we have all broken them, and so did our forefathers! Escaping the curse due to us or to our forefathers is totally impossible without the amazing love sacrifice of God Himself when He sent His only Son to be our *Kippurim* – our atonement or expiation sacrifice.

"The Messiah has redeemed us from the curse of the law, having become a curse for us (for it is written, "Cursed is everyone who hangs on a tree)."
—Galatians 3:13

The only way of escape out of a family curse is through faith in Yeshua, that is the *number one* step, and there is absolutely no way around it! I believe that every physical or mental illness that is called a "genetic" disease is an outcome of the family curse due to the sins of our ancestors. While medical science can help relieve some of the symptoms and even make the condition somehow tolerable, it has absolutely *no cure* for it. Yet the blood atonement of Yeshua brought radical healing to this impossible situation!

"He is despised and rejected by men, a Man of sorrows and acquainted with grief. And we hid, as it were, our faces from Him; He was despised, and we did not esteem Him. Surely He has borne our griefs and carried our sorrows; yet we esteemed Him stricken, Smitten by God, and afflicted. But He was wounded for our transgressions, He was bruised for our iniquities; the chastisement for our peace was upon Him, and by His stripes we are healed."

—Isaiah 53:3-5

Total Faith

Since Yeshua completely redeemed us, saved us and rescued us from the curse that we inherited due to the breaking of His Father's commandments, we need to trust His finished sacrifice and *believe* in His Word. This is our inheritance as believers in Yeshua – *total redemption*. We need to understand that He did not do this work halfway; when He was hanging on the Roman Cross in Jerusalem, He said, "It is finished," and then gave up his spirit. Everything needed for us to be freed from *both* sin and the outcome of sin (the curse!) was completely accomplished – there is nothing else to do besides put our *total faith* in His finished work!

Please do not believe for a moment that "genetical diseases" are your inheritance; however real they are and however bothersome and even dangerous, you have a better inheritance. You do not have to suffer the same fate as your ancestors! You can begin a new blood line through Yeshua's atoning blood, and the inheritance that Yeshua left for you is a *sound mind* and a *clean bill of health*. King David anticipating the blood atonement of Yeshua declared 1000 years before He came:

"Bless Yahveh, O my soul; And all that is within me, bless His holy name! Bless Yahveh, O my soul, and forget not all His benefits: Who forgives all your iniquities, Who heals all your diseases."

—Psalms 103:1-3

The only reason that you will claim "genetic diseases" as your inheritance is because of the *ignorance* of Yeshua's finished work or/and because of fear. Fear will keep you depressed and sick. The opposite of fear is a *sound mind*:

"For God has not given us a spirit of fear, but of power and of love and of a sound mind."

—2 Timothy 1:7

Practical steps to take

1. Acknowledge, confess and repent of your sins, and accept Yeshua as your Master, Savior and Healer. Forsake all other gods, religions, superstitious objects, good luck charms and mediators. Remember that there is only one that can mediate between you and Elohim, the God of Israel, that is Yeshua, the Son of God, who left His Divinity to become as a sinless man. He gave Himself for you and paid with His

own blood for you to be forgiven. Pray the following:

> Dear heavenly Father, I ask your forgiveness and repent for breaking your holy commandments. I also ask forgiveness on behalf of my ancestors up to the fifth generation for worshipping other gods in any way shape and form. Yes, Yeshua, I put my trust in you as my Master, Savior and Healer. Thank you for reconciling me with the Creator through your blood atonement and becoming my only mediator to Yahveh, God. You rose from the dead on the third day and you are alive; I will walk with You all my days and hereby forsake all other gods, religions, mediators, good luck charms and superstitious objects. I am Yours forever! Thank you for redeeming me from the curse due to my ancestors breaking of Your Father, Yahveh's commandments. Thank you for removing from off me all family curses and the so-called "genetic diseases," including depression and mental illness. Through You, I will praise YAH (God) forever! If you have done this in faith, congratulations, you have passed from death to life and from the curse to the blessing!

2. Begin to confess His Word on this matter. Make for yourself a "word prayer" with at least 5 Scriptures on this subject (some of them are mentioned in this article, and you can also use a concordance of the Bible). Speak these words

out loud to yourself, pray them, sing them, etc. Until you believe nothing else but what He said, this is the truth!

"Then Yeshua said to those Jews who believed Him, 'If you abide in My word, you are My disciples indeed. And you shall know the truth, and the truth shall make you free.'"

—John 8:31,32

3. Cleanse your home from all idolatry, superstition and ungodly religious objects, including books, jewels, home ornaments and clothes. You may need the help of someone that is more mature in the faith in order to recognize these. Ask Yeshua to guide you and to lead you to the right person to help you.

4. Go to a trusted minister of deliverance that is baptized in the Holy Spirit so he/she can pray with you against "familiar spirits" and/or spirits connected with occult, witchcraft, idolatry and the like. This is very important!

The majority of Yeshua's ministry in Israel was about casting out evil spirits and healing those that were oppressed of the devil. He left us, His believers, the same ministry:

"He who believes and is baptized will be saved; but he who does not believe will be condemned. And these signs will follow those who believe: In My name they will cast out demons; they will speak with new tongues."

—Mark 16:16, 17

5. Ask the above ministers to lay hands on you to be

baptized/immersed in the Holy Spirit with speaking in tongues (heavenly languages) like the Jewish disciples were in the Book of Acts. Exercise your new prayer language very often.

> "But you, beloved, building yourselves up on your most holy faith, praying in the Holy Spirit."
>
> —Jude 20

6. Follow the instructions given in chapters 1-4.

7. Submit to YAH (God) and resist the devil and he will flee from you (James 4:7). Exercise authority in the name of Yeshua against all spirits of confusion, depression and fear! Be firm! Pray the following:

> In the mighty name of Yeshua, I forbid any spirits of confusion, depression and fear from operating in and/or through me. I bind you and command you to leave me now! I command all my thoughts to be captives to Yeshua the Messiah, His Spirit and His Word. In Yeshua's name. Amen.

> *"Behold, I give you the authority to trample on serpents and scorpions, and over all the power of the enemy, and nothing shall by any means hurt you."*
>
> —Luke 10:19

8. Lead a life of prayer, study of YAH's (God's} Word and obedience to His Will.

9. By faith, obedience, forgiveness and holiness, keep all the doors to the devil and the kingdom of darkness tightly shut.

Go ahead! Be free from depression and live an abundant life as Yeshua promised!

"Beloved, I pray that you may prosper in all things and be in health, just as your soul prospers."

—3 John 2

CHAPTER 6
Trust in God will Remove Your Depression

"He who is of a proud heart stirs up strife, but he who trusts in Yahveh will be prospered."
—Proverbs 28:25

As we paraphrase the above verse from the original Hebrew, it will read as follows: *"He who is of a proud heart stirs up strife, but he who trusts in Yahveh will be fertilized."*

In other words, the humble ones that trust in and are dependent on the Almighty will suffer "stinking situations" that will fertilize their lives and bring their lives into abundance fruitfulness! Fertilizers are very strong in smell, but without them, we cannot get abundant crops. And it is the same in our lives, we will go through "hard to stomach" situations and everyone else will see that we are suffering; however, the purpose of these "stinking, fertilizing situations" is to bring us to fruitfulness, prosperity and abundance!

So many times we wonder: why is it that hard situations "hit" our lives? How can it be that we, being people of the Covenant, live through distresses, tragedies and disasters? How can it be that Israel has suffered so much after 2,000 years of exile in order to fulfill Yahveh's plan to reestablish her as a light unto the nations? So many times we get angry with Yah (God) and point a finger at Him for allowing hard things to happen in our lives. And what is worst, many have developed the culture of "Job's comforters" trying to find fault with whoever is suffering! "It must be his fault, they say. It is probably the sins of so and so, or the terrible sins of Israel that have brought this terrible predicament forth."

"Now as Yeshua passed by, He saw a man who was blind from birth. And His disciples asked Him, saying, 'Rabbi, who sinned, this man or his parents, that he was born blind?' Yeshua answered, 'Neither this man nor his parents sinned, but that the works of God should be revealed in him.'"

—John 9:1-3

It is always in the nature of man to point a finger, however every time that we point a finger to someone else, three fingers will be pointing at us – the Triune God Himself.

"For a righteous man may fall seven times and rise again, but the wicked shall fall by calamity."

—Proverbs 24:16

We need to understand that the Covenant People of God, be it Gentiles or Jews, will fall sometimes, yes, even seven times, which means "an unlimited amount of times," but they will rise again *every* time! However, the wicked will fall and will not rise up!

The difference between the wicked and the righteous is not that the righteous has no troubles or even prospers more than the wicked, no! The difference is in the response of the righteous during hardship. His response of faith and trust in Yah will cause him to rise up above the fallen wicked! Jeremiah said:

"Righteous are You, O Yahveh, when I plead with You; Yet let me talk with You about Your judgments. Why does the way of the wicked prosper? Why are those happy who deal so treacherously?"

—Jeremiah 12:1

The wicked will prosper for a time, but when trouble hits, he will be suddenly destroyed and that without a remedy.

If you are going through a hard situation and everyone can see your vulnerability, be encouraged today – you are being fertilized! You are being made fruitful and prosperous! It is not necessarily your sins that have brought this about, it may really be that your trust in Yah has brought this about! He has put His eye on you as a "fruitful land" and has decided to fertilize you so that you will be prosperous! If you have "Job's comforters" around you or "well-meaning critics," just thank them and Yah for they are part of your "fertilization." Eventually, everyone will also be able to see the gorgeous fruit in your life and glorify the Father in Heaven for your "sudden" prosperity and success. Only you will know the years of "fertilization" that you have gone through!

Keep yourself in love, in forgiveness and thankfulness, and do not lose sight of the vision for which purpose you are being "fertilized." Then the perfumed anointing of ADONAI will be in you and upon you mightily, and it will cause you to forget the "stink." Pray the following:

> Dear heavenly Father, thank you for "fertilizing" me that I may bring forth fruit in abundance. Please forgive me for doubting You during the hard times. I choose to trust You now and forever. In Yeshua's name. Amen.

"Looking unto Yeshua, the author and finisher of our faith, who for the joy that was set before Him endured the cross, despising the shame, and has sat down at the right hand of the throne of God."

—Hebrews 12:2

CHAPTER 7

"Love" – The Medication that Never Fails

"Though I speak with the tongues of men and of angels, but have not love, I have become sounding brass or a clanging cymbal. And though I have the gift of prophecy, and understand all mysteries and all knowledge, and though I have all faith, so that I could remove mountains, but have not love, I am nothing. And though I bestow all my goods to feed the poor, and though I give my body to be burned, but have not love, it profits me nothing. Love suffers long and is kind; love does not envy; love does not parade itself, is not puffed up; does not behave rudely, does not seek its own, is not provoked, thinks no evil; does not rejoice in iniquity, but rejoices in the truth; bears all things, believes all things, hopes all things, endures all things. Love

never fails. But whether there are prophecies, they will fail; whether there are tongues, they will cease; whether there is knowledge, it will vanish away. For we know in part and we prophesy in part. But when that which is perfect has come, then that which is in part will be done away When I was a child, I spoke as a child, I understood as a child, I thought as a child; but when I became a man, I put away childish things. For now we see in a mirror, dimly, but then face to face. Now I know in part, but then I shall know just as I also am known. And now abide faith, hope, love, these three; but the greatest of these is love."
—1 Corinthians 13

This chapter is here to encourage you that when you feel that all else has failed, there is only one thing that will never fail, and that is *love*. In Hebrew it is the word '*Ahavah*'. The word '*Ahavah*' is the most revealing word of the Hebrew language! Let me explain:

The first and the third letter form the word *Ab* with the letters *Alef* and *Bet*. In Hebrew, the whole alphabet is called *Alef Bet* and also the foundation of anything is called the *Alef Bet*. Without the *Alef Bet*, the first two letters of the Hebrew alphabet, we have no foundation for the language!

The letters *Alef Bet* form the word *Ab* or *Av*, which means *father*. Without the love of a *father*, there is no foundation to life! Most of the people that suffer from depression and especially suicidal depression have lacked the stabilizing presence and love of their father, this the *Alef Bet*, the *a,b,c*, or the foundation of life is missing.

The second and last letters of *Ahavah* is the letter *Heh* or *h*. That letter is always used to write the name of ADONAI, so *Heh* means God. But the *Heh* represents the *breathe* of God or the *Ruach* ADONAI, who in Hebrew is a feminine form. Yes, Holy Spirit in Hebrew is feminine. So, the *Heh* represents the "mother spirit" and in this case the love of a mother, the life bringer. The word *Ahavah* represents a perfect balance between the masculine and the feminine attributes of God. Please remember that the Creator created *Adam* in His image, "male and female created He them," so He has both male and female in Him.

"Then God said, 'Let Us make man in Our image, according to Our likeness; let them have dominion over the fish of the sea, over the birds of the air, and over the cattle, over all the earth and over every creeping thing that creeps on the earth.' So God created man in His own image; in the image of God He created him; male and female He created them."

—Genesis 1:26-27

That is why a married couple, a father and a mother, are to be the foundation for a healthy life for the child.

Ungodly parents, abusive parents, divorced parents, etc., are the cause for the most instability in the life of their children! Nearly every mental problem in a child can be linked to the condition of his parents. Are they holy, healthy, stable, loving, or are they not? A child experiences the love of God through his/her parents; if they are unable to give that, their children will experience many struggles such as depression and even suicide.

Though both parents are equally needed and complementary in order to demonstrate the love of God, the lack of proper fatherhood is the most detrimental because the bloodline of the children is communicated through the fathers. That is the reason why in the Holy Scriptures, we mostly know who the father is and not who the mother is. The lack of fatherhood in this generation is appalling! And it is definitely a plan of Satan by destroying the very fiber of society – the family unit!

We could easily ask ourselves, "what can we do now?" So many of us were raised with absent fathers, whether alcoholic, abusive, selfish, workaholics, divorced or non-existent altogether. So, the predicament for our generation and the next is mental problems, emotional problems, depression and suicide! And indeed, these are unfortunately and steadily on the rise! But I have good news for you! There is a way out of this, and it is *both* a miracle and a process!

Ahavah – Love Is A Choice!

If you are among those that were not properly parented, welcome to the "club." You are not alone; this is a general problem. You can, as of today, make a choice to change your whole outlook on life from victim to victor! You can choose *Ahavah* right now by choosing to give full entrance to the Messiah Yeshua into your heart and life and by deciding to imitate Him.

"How God anointed Yeshua of Nazareth with the Holy Spirit and with power, who went about doing good and healing all who were oppressed by the devil, for God was with Him."

—Acts 10:38

Yeshua is the *fruit of Ahavah*; He is the product of the Father in Heaven, impregnating Miriam, a young Jewish virgin with the Holy Spirit, the Ruach (the feminine mother side of Yahveh). The Oneness of God conceived a Son in the womb of Miriam as prophesied by the Hebrew prophet Isaiah.

"Therefore Yahveh Himself will give you a sign: Behold, the virgin shall conceive and bear a Son, and shall call His name Immanuel."

—Isaiah 7:14

Yeshua is the *love*, the *Ahavah* of God incarnate, made flesh. He proved Himself to be LOVE all the way up to His execution and sacrifice on a Roman Cross in order to pay for our sins. He did the ultimate act of love; He gave His soul a ransom for our sins! When we accept Yeshua's love sacrifice, the *Ahavah* of His Father enters us through the Ruach, the Spirit of God and washes away all orphanhood from us. We become then children of God newly born of the love of God. That is the miracle!

"For God so loved the world that He gave His only begotten Son, that whoever believes in Him should not perish but have everlasting life."

—John 3:16

Now the process begins, the process of retraining our minds to believe in love and to choose love in our thinking, in our feelings and in our actions. We need to choose the Ahavah lifestyle daily and against all odds and circumstances. Love is always the *best* choice in every situation, and it cannot fail! The only one that failed among the 12 apostles of Yeshua was Judas Iscariot who lived and fellowshipped with love Himself for over three years. He chose to betray and reject love and ended up committing suicide! There was no more hope for him because he had known love intimately and still chose wickedness, money, fame and hatred instead. Rejecting God's love in the person of Yeshua is most particularly detrimental for those that have had a lack of *Ahavah* parenting as they do not have what it takes to cope with this life – sooner or later they break! Most people did not enjoy the blessing of Judas Iscariot that knew love intimately and so most people that try to commit suicide, they do so because of the unbearable pain they suffer. "If they knew love, they knew Yeshua they would shift that unbearable pain to Him who took all of their sin and also all of their pain!" (—Isaiah 53)

"Surely He has borne our griefs And carried our sorrows; Yet we esteemed Him stricken, Smitten by God, and afflicted. But He was wounded for our transgressions, He was bruised for our iniquities; The chastisement for our peace was upon Him, And by His stripes we are healed. All we like sheep have gone astray; We have turned, every one, to his own way; And Yahveh has laid on Him the iniquity of us all."

—Isaiah 53:4-6

And these are the good news that *Ahavah* Himself took all of your sin and all of your pain. There is no need to escape pain through depression or suicide – just give it up to Him that already took it for you and breathe *love* in; His endless, unconditional all-encompassing *love* and *compassion* for you! Do not reject or be afraid of such love any longer, accept Him fully and let Him teach you *Ahavah*! Then make *Ahavah* your choice *forever*!

A Life Changing Prayer

Yeshua, come into my heart and life, be my father and my mother, fill me with your Ahavah and lead me in love's way. I forgive all that have wronged me; ask and receive your forgiveness for all my wrongdoings, and I am yours forever!

Choose love, choose life, and be made whole!

EPILOGUE
Vessels of Clay

*"But we have this treasure in earthen vessels
that the excellence of the power may be of God
and not of us."*
—2 Corinthians 4:7

In the midst of a two-day retreat with my precious husband on the Mountains of Upper Galilee, in a place that only a few days earlier had suffered from the Hizbollah onslaught of Katiusha rockets, I received the following:

Elohim made us to be "Vessels of Clay" and highly breakable!

I am sure that in the back of our minds we all know that, but it is different to know it in our minds than to have a revelation on it. This was a revelation! I have been meditating on the fact that so many people suffer from depression and on the emotional frailty of this present generation. Past generations seem to have been stronger emotionally and able to stand a lot more hardship. This seemingly "puffed cream generation" tends to have breakdowns more often. Life is a lot more stressed, fast paced and demanding. Communication abounds to the point of obsessiveness. The "rat race" is at its worst and with it the escalation of divorces, single parent families, absent fathers, etc. The use of drugs and any kind of "emotional anesthetics" is at an all times high; people just want to numb the pain that does not seem to go away. It would be nice if I could report that in the "church" people suffer less from all this, yet I would be lying or seriously mistaken. The ones that come to Yeshua are those that need a doctor. However, many times there is no real doctor to be found in His House. The healing and the *retraining* of the mind is one of the most important End Time Ministries. Broken vessels are unusable because

They cannot hold any substance; they leak, and so in times past, broken vessels had to be discarded. However, praise be to Yah who is so merciful! He is not going to discard an entire generation of broken clay vessels. He is going to "fix" it! He is fixing to release some amazing ministries of *restoration,* and the world will be divided between those that are broken clay vessels and between those that will restore them in order to recruit them to restore others! In the midst of all this we will need to remember that restored vessels have weak points in the place of their past breaking, therefore, the only way that they can make it is as long as the Master Potter uses them. Any time that they are sold for the use of any other master besides the Master Potter, they will break into million pieces! The Master Potter is Yeshua, and as long as we submit to His hand in everything, though we are weak, though we are *highly breakable*, we will stand and be *whole*. Any time that we choose to get out of His hand and serve anyone rather than Him or any cause rather than His kingdom cause, we will fall apart.

This generation can stand no more pressure! It has had all the sin that it can take, all the stress that it can stand and all the selfishness that it can muster; it is time for a radical change of course for an entire generation! People are now asking the question, "What now? Where are we headed to?" There are many "apocalyptic films" because everyone is sensing that we have come to the Crossroads of History! It is time for repentance and for a turning! Those that will arise and shine during these times need to have answers, if not the broken vessels of this generation will turn more and more to New Age and occult and eventually be part of the great deception of the New World Order that is already here.

Vessels of Clay Will Minister to Vessels of Clay

The difference between human and human and vessel and vessel is not the outer substance but rather the "inner substance." Every person upon the face of the earth, including the
    toughest "oil tycoon," is made out of clay and is *highly breakable*! It really takes only a "straw to break the camel's

back" as the saying goes, and you never know when that "straw" of a circumstance is going to hit your back! No, the difference between human and human is not in any other but in the *contents* of that human. Those that are filled with Yeshua have a *treasure*, yet that treasure called the Holy Spirit is in "earthen" or Clay Vessel. For us to be able to stand the pressure from within, the pressure of the treasure, and the pressure from without life's circumstances, we must realize the following:

We Are Very Needy People!
And we need all of His compassion and mercy. Yes. We need all of His strength, beyond our capabilities. We need to realize how weak we are so that we can be made strong in Him. We need to realize that He pities even the one that thinks to be Himself a great "powerhouse." He knows that we are but clay and highly breakable! The moment that we break, the treasure leaks out, so we need to be repaired quickly. That is why Jeremiah the Prophet said:

"Is there no balm in Gilead, Is there no physician there? Why then is there no recovery For the health of the daughter of my people?"

—Jeremiah 8:22

Earlier on in the same chapter, he had made the following statement:

"For they have healed the hurt of the daughter of My people slightly, Saying, 'Peace, peace!' When there is no peace."
—Jeremiah 8:11

He knew full well that the wound that sin and rebellion leaves is too deep a wound to cure with only a band aid called "peace." There is a need for a balm and for a physician. The balm is the Word mixed with the Holy Spirit:

His Word, His Torah and Spirit makes for the best balm in the world. It cleanses with truth (word), and it heals with Ruach – Spirit!

Today *both* Israel and the Church worldwide are in need of the *true* balm of His Word with His Spirit, and many of YAH's Vessels of Clay are to be filled with this precious ointment. The good news is that as we "house" this marvelous balm of healing, it will heal us first! A balm is thick, not like oil that is "runny," and so even imperfect vessels, like me and maybe you that is reading this word, are able to "house" it inside of us. As we begin to give it away, as we touch it to dispense it, He will be healing us *first*. That is great news!

The more that you are restored to the full canon of the Holy Scripture, to the Torah and His unchanging Word in both Covenants, and you mix this with the oil of the Holy Spirit, this miraculous balm will be formed in you! You will be a "physician" to heal others. To give them answers, to dispense true love, and at the same time you will be made whole by administering it.

Right after Paul states that we have this treasure in clay vessels, he goes on to say that he is suffering great tribulation and he could break but he does not, because He is in the hands of the Master Potter!

"We are hard-pressed on every side, yet not crushed; we are perplexed, but not in despair; persecuted, but not forsaken; struck down, but not destroyed."

—2 Corinthians 4:8-9

This Healing Balm from Gilead (called also Golan) is from the North of Israel. In Psalms 133, the Psalmist talks about this precious oil coming from Mount Hermon who is also in the Golan Heights, the most threatened region of Israel! He talks about the precious oil of *unity* (Hebrew, *yachad*) – when the whole of Israel is in one accord and with singleness of vision, then Yahveh will bless with revival and with eternal life!

"Behold, how good and how pleasant it is For brethren to dwell together in unity! It is like the precious oil upon the head, Running down on the beard, The beard of Aaron, Running down on the edge of his garments. It is like the dew of Hermon, Descending upon the mountains of Zion; For there Yahveh commanded the blessing— Life forevermore."

—Psalms 133

As we become *yachad*, united with singleness of vision that it is time for the restoration of all things, the Jewish roots of the faith, the Holy Feasts, the Shabbat, the holiness and of course *Israel*, we will then experience this *oil* that comes from the highest "Mount Hermon," from the Throne of Glory Himself! And as we "mix" it with the Ruach (the Holy Spirit) it will form the *Balm of Gilead* that this generation needs.

Until now we only spoke about the importance of the *Anointing*; from now on we will speak about the *Balm of Healing, the Balm of Gilead*. And this precious *balm* will be dispensed out of very imperfect Vessels of Clay like you and I that love His Word, His commandments, instructions and promises, as well as the manifestations and demonstrations of His Holy Spirit!

"Now to Him who is able to do exceedingly abundantly above all that we ask or think, according to the power that works in us, to Him be glory in the church by the Messiah Yeshua to all generations, forever and ever. Amen."

—Ephesians 3:20,21

Thank you for being *yachad* (united) with us as we cooperate with the Physician and the Master Potter in the preparation of Clay Vessels that will dispense the healing Balm of Gilead to this broken generation. Both in Israel, in the church and in the Nations. Your prayers, your friendship and your financial support in this very urgently needed task, helps us Clay Vessels to go on in spite of our "breakability."

Shalom (Healing, Wholeness and Wellbeing) in Yeshua.
Archbishop Dr. Dominiquae Bierman

CONNECT WITH US

Other Books by Archbishop Dr. Dominiquae Bierman

Order now online: www.kad-esh.org/shop/

The MAP Revolution (Free E-Book)
Find Out Why Revival Does Not Come... Yet!

The Identity Theft
The Return of the 1st Century Messiah

From Sickology to a Healthy Logic
The Product of 18 Years Walking Through Psychiatric Hospitals

ATG: Addicts Turning to God
The Biblical Way to Handle Addicts and Addictions

The Healing Power of the Roots
It's a Matter of Life or Death!

Grafted In
It's Time to Take the Nation's!

Sheep Nations
It's Time to Take the Nations!

Restoring the Glory: The Original Way
The Ancient Paths Rediscovered

Stormy Weather
Judgment Has Already Begun,
Revival is Knocking at the Door

Yeshua is the Name
The Important Restoration of the Original
Hebrew Name of the Messiah

The Bible Cure for Africa and the Nations
The Key to the Restoration of All Africa

The Key of Abraham
The Blessing or the Curse?

Yes!
The Dramatic Salvation of Archbishop
Dr. Dominiquae Bierman

Eradicating the Cancer of Religion
Hint: All People Have It

Restoration of Holy Giving
Releasing the True 1,000 Fold Blessing

Vision Negev
The Awesome Restoration of the Sephardic Jews

The Woman Factor by Rabbi Baruch Bierman
Freedom From Womanphobia

The Revival of the Third Day (Free E-Book)
The Return to Yeshua the Jewish Messiah

Music Albums
www.kad-esh.org/shop/

The Key of Abraham

Abba Shebashamayim

Uru

Retorno

Get Equipped & Partner with Us

Global Revival MAP (GRM) Israeli Bible School
Take the most comprehensive video Bible school online that focuses on dismantling replacement theology.
For more information or to order, please contact us:
www.grmbibleschool.com
grm@dominiquaebierman.com

United Nations for Israel Movement

We invite you to join us as a member and partner with $25 a month, which supports the advancing of this End time vision that will bring true unity to the body of the Messiah. We will see the One New Man form, witness the restoration of Israel, and take part in the birthing of SHEEP NATIONS. Today is an exciting time to be serving Him!

www.unitednationsforisrael.org

info@unitednationsforisrael.org

Global Re-Education Initiative (GRI) Against Anti-Semitism

Discover the Jewishness of the Messiah and defeat Christian anti-Semitism with this online video course to see revival in your nation!

www.against-antisemitism.com

info@against-antisemitism.com

Join Our Annual Israel Tours

Travel through the Holy Land and watch the Hebrew Holy Scriptures come alive.

www.kad-esh.org/tours-and-events/

To Send Offerings to Support our Work

Your help keeps this mission of restoration going far and wide.

www.kad-esh.org/donations

CONTACT US

Archbishop Dr. Dominiquae & Rabbi Baruch Bierman

Kad-Esh MAP Ministries | www.kad-esh.org

info@kad-esh.org

United Nations for Israel | www.unitednationsforisrael.org

info@unitednationsforisrael.org

Zion's Gospel Press | shalom@zionsgospel.com

52 Tuscan Way, Ste 202-412, 32092 St. Augustine Florida, USA

+1-972-301-7087

www.ingramcontent.com/pod-product-compliance
Lightning Source LLC
Chambersburg PA
CBHW022231080526
44577CB00005B/144